HSC
Health & Safety
Commission

Approved guide to the classification and labelling of substances and preparations dangerous for supply
(Third edition)

Chemicals (Hazard Information and Packaging for Supply) (Amendment) Regulations 1997

CHIP 97

GUIDANCE ON REGULATIONS

L100

HSE BOOKS

First published 1993
Second edition 1994
Third edition 1997

ISBN 0 7176 1366 6

Contents

Notice of Approval

The Health and Safety Commission has on 25 March 1997 approved the publication of this document, *Approved Classification and Labelling Guide (Third edition)*, for the purposes of the Chemicals (Hazard Information and Packaging for Supply) Regulations 1994 as amended by the Chemicals (Hazard Information and Packaging for Supply) (Amendment) Regulations 1997. This Approved Classification and Labelling Guide (Third edition) shall have effect from 7 July 1997, which is the date on which the 1997 Regulations come into force, and on that date the *Approved Classification and Labelling Guide (Second edition)* (approved by the Health and Safety Commission on 2 November 1994 for the purposes of the Chemicals (Hazard Information and Packaging for Supply) Regulations 1994) shall cease to have effect.

Signed

T A GATES
Secretary to the Health and Safety Commission

6 June 1997

Preface

This Approved Classification and Labelling Guide (Third edition) is based on EC Directive 93/21/EEC as amended by 96/54/EC, which together set out Annex VI to the Dangerous Substances Directive, 67/548/EEC. The purpose of this Annex is to provide a harmonised basis for the classification and labelling of dangerous substances and preparations in member states.

The Chemicals (Hazard Information and Packaging for Supply) Regulations 1994 as amended by the Chemicals (Hazard Information and Packaging for Supply) (Amendment) Regulations 1996 and by the Chemicals (Hazard Information and Packaging for Supply) (Amendment) Regulations 1997 (collectively referred to as 'CHIP') impose requirements by reference to this Guide and to that extent it is legally binding.

The Approved Classification and Labelling Guide (3rd edition) is one of four documents supporting CHIP. The other three documents are: The Approved Code of Practice *Safety data sheets for substances and preparations dangerous for supply (2nd Edition)*; the *Approved Supply List (3rd Edition)* and *Approved Supply List Supplement*.

Introduction

1 This Approved Guide sets out the general principles of classification and labelling for supply as required by the Chemicals (Hazard Information and Packaging for Supply) Regulations 1994 as amended (CHIP). It is addressed to manufacturers, importers and other suppliers who have responsibilities for the classification and labelling of dangerous substances and preparations. In practice, classification will be carried out by an individual, and such a person should be competent to perform the task.* This third edition of the Approved Guide introduces three main changes:

(a) a new R-phrase (R65) and criteria for chemicals which could cause lung damage if swallowed (the aspiration hazard) (paragraphs 48 and 155 and new text for S62 in Appendix 1);

(b) new criteria for the classification of chemicals as sensitisers (paragraphs 58 to 76); and

(c) a labelling derogation for propane, butane and liquified petroleum gas (LPG) (paragraphs 152 to 154).

2 The purpose of classification is to identify the properties of substances and preparations that may constitute a hazard during normal handling and use. It is important to note that there is a difference between hazard (ie the inherent properties of a chemical) and risk (ie the probability of the hazardous properties of the chemical causing harm to people or the environment). Classification in this Approved Guide is about identification of the hazard not the risk. The properties considered are:

(a) for ***substances*** - physico-chemical, health and environmental properties; and

(b) for ***preparations*** - physico-chemical and health properties.

Once a substance or a preparation has been classified under regulation 5(4) of CHIP by application of the criteria in paragraphs 21 to 133, the supply label required by regulation 9 of CHIP is derived using the criteria in paragraphs 134 to 151.

3 The supply label is intended to provide a primary means by which people at work and the general public are given essential information about dangerous substances and preparations. It draws the attention of users to the inherent hazards of such materials so that the necessary precautionary measures can be taken. The label may also serve to draw attention to more comprehensive product information on safety such as the supplier's safety data sheet.

4 The label should take account of all potential hazards that are likely to arise in normal handling and use of a dangerous substance or preparation in the form in which it is supplied, although not necessarily in any different form in which it may ultimately be used, eg diluted. The information on the label includes (regulation 9 of CHIP):

(a) symbols and general indications of danger which highlight the most severe hazards;

(b) standard risk phrases, which specify the hazards arising from (a) and from other dangerous properties; and

(c) standard safety phrases which give advice on the necessary precautions.

* In this context a competent person would be one who has the necessary knowledge and experience to perform the task of classification.

5 Regulations 9 and 10 of the Carriage of Dangerous Goods by Road and Rail (Classification, Packaging and Labelling) Regulations 1994* show how, under certain circumstances, the labelling details for supply and for carriage may be combined.

Scope

6 This Approved Guide applies to dangerous substances and preparations as defined in CHIP, and should be read in the context of those Regulations. In particular, the criteria in this Approved Guide should be used for the classification and labelling for supply of:

(a) ***substances***, except those listed in the Approved Supply List for which agreed classifications and labels are already specified. New substances as defined in the Notification of New Substances Regulations 1993 (NONS)† are included, whether or not they are notifiable within the meaning of these Regulations; and

(b) ***preparations***.

7 Supply labels derived by a manufacturer or supplier in accordance with this Approved Guide for a substance not yet listed in the Approved Supply List remain valid until the substance is listed in the Approved Supply List, or until a decision has been taken not to classify and label it in accordance with an agreed European procedure.

Data for classification and labelling

8 For ***substances***, the data required for classification and labelling can be obtained from a number of different sources. In the case of notified new substances, most of the necessary data should already be available in the 'base set' provided under the Notification of New Substances Regulations 1993. The classification and labelling should be reviewed, however, if further information becomes available under Level 1 or 2. For other substances the necessary data may come from:

(a) the results of previous tests;

(b) information required by international rules on the transport of dangerous goods;

(c) reference works or scientific and technical literature; or

(d) practical experience.

9 For ***preparations*** the physico-chemical and health effect data required for classification and labelling may be obtained by application of the test methods specified in Annex V of Directive 67/548/EEC.‡ In the case of health effects, the classification may also be obtained by application of the conventional method as set out in Schedule 3 of the CHIP Regulations. Note, however, that the conventional method must always be used for the evaluation of carcinogenicity, mutagenicity and reproductive toxicity.

* SI No 1994/669
† SI No 1993/3050
‡ Annex V to this Directive has been adopted in the UK as an Approved Code of Practice under section 16(1) of the Health and Safety at Work etc Act 1974. The Notice of Approval is reproduced at Appendix 2 to this Guide.

10 The criteria in this Approved Guide are directly applicable when the data has been obtained from test methods equivalent to those described in Annex V of Directive 67/548/EEC. In other cases, the available data should be assessed by comparing the test methods used with those in Annex V of Directive 67/548/EEC and by applying the criteria in this Guide to determine the classification and label.

Animal tests

11 The performance of animal tests to establish experimental data is subject to the Animals (Scientific Procedures) Act 1986, which implements Directive 86/609/EEC, regarding the protection of animals used for experimental purposes.

Application of the criteria in this Guide

12 Classification of substances and preparations should include consideration of all the physico-chemical and toxicological properties covered in this Approved Guide (paragraphs 21 to 35 and 36 to 120 respectively). In addition, classification of substances should include consideration of ecotoxicological properties (paragraphs 121 to 133). Risk phrases should be selected to ensure that all the potential dangers identified in classification are properly reflected on the label. When selecting symbols and risk phrases, it is important, therefore, to consider in turn each of the criteria in this Approved Guide.

13 The criteria in this Approved Guide are also applicable to gaseous substances and preparations in so far as they are subject to the packaging and labelling provisions of CHIP. Gaseous preparations are covered explicitly in paragraphs 153 to 162.

Classification of substances containing impurities, additives or individual constituents

14 Where a substance contains an impurity or additive, or an individual constituent has been identified, its presence should be taken into account in the classification if the concentration of the impurity, additive or individual constituent is equal to or exceeds:

(a) the concentration of 0.1% for substances classified as very toxic, toxic, carcinogenic (Category 1 or 2), and mutagenic (Category 1 or 2);

(b) the concentration of 0.5% for substances classified as toxic to reproduction (Category 1 or 2);

(c) the concentration of 1% for substances classified as harmful, corrosive, irritant, sensitising or carcinogenic (Category 3), and mutagenic (Category 3);

(d) the concentration of 5% for substances classified as toxic to reproduction (Category 3);

unless lower values have been specified in the Approved Supply List.

15 With the exception of those substances listed in the Approved Supply List, classification of substances containing impurities, additives or individual constituents for physico-chemical properties and health effects should be carried out in accordance with the requirements of Schedule 3 of the CHIP Regulations. Classification for effects dangerous for the environment should be carried out in accordance to the criteria specified in paragraphs 121 to 133 of this Guide.

16 Labelling for these substances should be carried out in accordance with regulation 9(3) and Schedule 6 Part I of CHIP, as if the substance was a preparation.

17 In the case of asbestos, this general rule does not apply until a concentration limit has been set in the Approved Supply List. Substances in which asbestos is present should be classified and labelled according to the principles in regulation 5(4) of CHIP.

Preparations or substances containing impurities, additives or individual constituents which are used as constituents of another preparation

18 The labelling of such preparations should be in accordance with regulation 9(3) of CHIP. However, in certain cases, the information on the label of the preparation or substance described in paragraph 14 may be insufficient to enable other manufacturers who wish to use it as a constituent of their own preparation(s) to carry out the classification and labelling of their preparation(s) correctly. In these cases, the person established within the European Community responsible for placing the original preparation or substance on the market, whether it be the manufacturer, importer or distributor, should supply upon justified request and as soon as possible all necessary data concerning the dangerous substances present to enable correct classification and labelling of the new preparation. These data are also necessary to enable the person responsible for supplying the new preparation to comply with other requirements of CHIP.

Source

19 This Approved Classification and Labelling Guide follows closely the European Commission's 'Labelling Guide', ie Annex VI of Directive 67/548/EEC. Where appropriate, references to EC Directives have been changed to the corresponding national provisions.

20 The classification and labelling details derived in accordance with this Approved Classification and Labelling Guide may need to be revised from time to time as the EC classification system for dangerous substances and preparations evolves and as more information on hazards becomes available.

Classification on the basis of physico-chemical properties

Criteria for classification, choice of symbols, indication of danger and choice of risk phrases

21 In general the test methods for explosive, oxidising and flammable properties set out in Annex V of Directive 67/548/EEC give specific criteria for classification under the physico-chemical properties defined in Schedule 1 of the CHIP Regulations.

22 However, certain of the test methods listed in Part III of Schedule 1 of CHIP may not be suitable in certain circumstances, as they can give widely differing results. Care should be taken, therefore, to apply the most appropriate test to the particular substance or preparation being classified. Advice on the correct test method to use can be sought on a case by case basis by contacting the HSE's Health Directorate (HD) D4, Magdalen House, Stanley Precinct, Bootle, Merseyside L20 3QZ.

23 If adequate information is available to demonstrate in practice that the physico-chemical properties of substances and preparations (apart from organic peroxides) are different from those revealed by the test methods in Annex V of Directive 67/548/EEC, then such substances and preparations should be classified according to the hazard (if any) they present to those handling the substances and preparations or to other people.

24 Full testing of preparations for explosive, oxidising and flammable properties may not be necessary if none of the constituent substances possess such properties - see paragraph 3 of Part I of Schedule 3 of the CHIP Regulations.

25 Notwithstanding the criteria in paragraphs 30 to 33, substances and preparations in the form of aerosols should be subject to the flammability criteria set out in Part II of Schedule 1 of the CHIP Regulations.

Explosive

26 Substances and preparations should be classified as explosive and assigned the corresponding symbol 'E' with the indication of danger 'explosive' in accordance with the results of the tests in Annex V of Directive 67/548/EEC and in so far as the substances and preparations are explosive as supplied. One risk phrase is obligatory and should be assigned as follows:

R2 *Risk of explosion by shock, friction, fire or other sources of ignition*

Substances and preparations including certain organic peroxides but excepting those assigned R3.

R3 *Extreme risk of explosion by shock, friction, fire or other sources of ignition*

Substances and preparations which are particularly sensitive such as picric acid salts or PETN.

Oxidising

27 Substances and preparations should be classified as oxidising and assigned the corresponding symbol 'O' with the indication of danger 'oxidising' in accordance with the results of the tests in Annex V of Directive 67/548/EEC. One risk phrase is obligatory. It should be assigned on the basis of the test results but subject to the following:

R7 *May cause fire*

Organic peroxides which have flammable properties even when not in contact with other combustible material.

R8 *Contact with combustible material may cause fire*

Other oxidising substances and preparations, including inorganic peroxides, which may cause fire or enhance the risk of fire when in contact with combustible material.

R9 *Explosive when mixed with combustible material*

Other substances and preparations, including inorganic peroxides which become explosive when mixed with combustible materials, eg certain chlorates.

Comments regarding peroxides

28 For the oxidising properties, the existing methods in Annex V of Directive 67/548/EEC cannot be applied to organic peroxides. For substances, organic peroxides are classified as oxidising on the basis of their structure (eg R-O-O-H; R1-O-O-R2). Preparations should be classified using the calculation method based on the presence of active oxygen shown in paragraphs 160 and 161. Any organic peroxide or preparation thereof is classified as oxidising, unless the peroxide or its formulation contains:

(a) not more than 5% of organic peroxides; or

(b) not more than 0.5% available oxygen from the organic peroxides, when containing not more than 5% hydrogen peroxide.

Liquid oxidisers

29 Note that there is currently no recommended or agreed test for liquid oxidisers. Advice on classifying liquid oxidisers can be sought on a case by case basis by contacting the HSE's Technology and Health Sciences Directorate (HD) D4, Magdalen House, Stanley Precinct, Bootle, Merseyside L20 3QZ.

Extremely flammable

30 Substances and preparations should be classified as extremely flammable and assigned the corresponding symbol 'F+' with the indication of danger 'extremely flammable' in accordance with the results of the tests in Part III of Schedule 1 of the CHIP Regulations, or where appropriate in Annex V of Directive 67/548/EEC (see also paragraph 22). The risk phrase should be assigned as follows:

R12 *Extremely flammable*

Liquid substances and preparations which have a flash point lower than 0°C and a boiling point (or, in case of a boiling range the initial boiling point) lower than or equal to 35°C.

Gaseous substances and preparations which are flammable in contact with air at ambient temperature and pressure.

Highly flammable

31 Substances and preparations should be classified as highly flammable and assigned the corresponding symbol 'F' with the indication of danger 'highly flammable' in accordance with the results of the tests referred to in paragraph 30. Risk phrases should be assigned as follows:

R11 *Highly flammable*

Solid substances and preparations which may readily catch fire after brief contact with a source of ignition and which continue to burn or to be consumed after removal of the source of ignition.

Liquid substances and preparations having a flash point below 21°C but which are not extremely flammable.

R15 *Contact with water liberates extremely flammable gases*

Substances and preparations which, in contact with water or damp air, evolve extremely flammable gases in dangerous quantities, at a minimum rate of 1 litre/kg/hr.

R17 *Spontaneously flammable in air*

Substances and preparations which may become hot and finally catch fire in contact with air at ambient temperature without any input of energy.

Flammable

32 Substances and preparations should be classified as flammable in accordance with the results of the tests referred to in paragraph 30. The risk phrases should be assigned as follows:

R10 *Flammable*

For liquid substances and preparations having a flash point equal to or greater than 21°C, and less than or equal to 55°C.

33 However, the following need not be classified as flammable:

(a) a liquid, which when tested at 55°C in the manner described in Schedule 2 of the Highly Flammable Liquids and Liquefied Petroleum Gases Regulations 1972, does not support combustion;

(b) a preparation which has been shown in practice not to support combustion, so long as there is no reason to fear risks to those handling these preparations or to other people.

Other physico-chemical properties

34 Additional risk phrases should be assigned to substances and preparations which have been classified by virtue of paragraphs 26 to 33 or by paragraphs 46 to 133, in accordance with the following criteria:

R1 *Explosive when dry*

For explosive substances and preparations supplied in solution or in a wetted form, eg nitro-cellulose with more than 12.6% nitrogen.

R4 *Forms very sensitive explosive metallic compounds*

For substances and preparations which may form sensitive explosive metallic derivatives, eg picric acid, styphnic acid.

R5 *Heating may cause an explosion*

For thermally unstable substances and preparations not classified as explosive, eg perchloric acid >50%.

R6 *Explosive with or without contact with air*

For substances and preparations which are unstable at ambient temperatures, eg acetylene.

R7 *May cause fire*

For reactive substances and preparations, eg fluorine, sodium hydrosulphite.

R14 *Reacts violently with water*

For substances and preparations which react violently with water, eg acetyl chloride, alkali metals, titanium tetrachloride.

R16 *Explosive when mixed with oxidising substances*

For substances and preparations which react explosively with an oxidising agent, eg red phosphorus.

R18 *In use, may form flammable/explosive vapour-air mixture*

For preparations not in themselves classified as flammable, which contain volatile components which are flammable in air.

R19 *May form explosive peroxides*

For substances and preparations which may form explosive peroxides during storage, eg diethyl ether, 1,4-dioxan.

R30 *Can become highly flammable in use*

For preparations not in themselves classified as flammable, which may become flammable due to the loss of non-flammable volatile components.

R44 *Risk of explosion if heated under confinement*

For substances and preparations not in themselves classified as explosive in accordance with paragraph 26 but which may nevertheless display explosive properties in practice if heated under sufficient confinement. For example, certain substances which would decompose explosively if heated in a steel drum do not show this effect if heated in less strong containers.

35 For other additional risk phrases see paragraph 119.

Classification on the basis of health effects

Criteria for classification, choice of symbols, indication of danger and choice of risk phrases

36 Classification is concerned with both the acute and long-term effects of substances and preparations, whether resulting from a single instance of exposure or from repeated or prolonged exposure.

37 If adequate evidence is available to demonstrate in practice that the toxic effect of a substance or preparation on man is, or is likely to be, different from that suggested by the experimental results obtained in animal tests or by the application of the conventional method in Part I of Schedule 3 of the CHIP Regulations, then the substance or preparation should be classified according to its toxicity in man. However, tests on man should be discouraged and should not normally be used to negate positive animal data.

38 ***Substances*** should be classified on the basis of available experimental data in accordance with the scheme set out in paragraphs 46 to 120. This scheme covers:

(a) acute lethal effects - paragraphs 46, 47 and 48;

(b) non-lethal irreversible effects after a single exposure - paragraphs 46, 47 and 48;

(c) severe effects after repeated or prolonged exposure - paragraphs 47 and 48;

(d) corrosive effects - paragraphs 55 and 56;

(e) irritant effects - paragraphs 57 to 60;

(f) sensitising effects - paragraphs 61 to 76;

(g) carcinogenic, mutagenic and reproductive toxicity effects - paragraphs 77 to 118;

(h) other toxicological properties - paragraph 119.

39 ***Preparations*** should be classified:

(a) in the absence of experimental data, by application of the conventional method in Part I of Schedule 3 of the CHIP Regulations. In this case the classification should be based on the individual concentration limits taken either:

  (i) from the Approved Supply List; or

  (ii) from Part II of Schedule 3 of the CHIP Regulations if the substance or substances do not appear in the Approved Supply List or appear in it without concentration limits; or

(b) where experimental data are available in accordance with the scheme in paragraph 38 with the exception of carcinogenic, mutagenic and toxic to reproduction properties, which must be evaluated by the conventional method in Part I of Schedule 3 of the CHIP Regulations.

40 Whichever method is used for the evaluation of the danger of a preparation, all the dangerous effects on health as defined in Part I of Schedule 3 of the CHIP Regulations must be taken into consideration.

41 When the classification is to be established from experimental results obtained in animal tests, the results should have validity for man in that the tests reflect, in an appropriate way, the risks to man.

42 The acute oral toxicity of substances or preparations placed on the market may be established either by a method permitting assessment of the LD_{50} value, or by determining the discriminating dose (the fixed dose procedure).

43 The discriminating dose is the dose which causes evident toxicity but not mortality and must be one of the four dosage levels specified in Annex V of Directive 67/548/EEC (5, 50, 500, or 2000 mg/kg/body weight).

44 The concept 'evident toxicity' is used to designate toxic effects after exposure to the substance tested, which are so severe that exposure to the next highest fixed dose would probably lead to mortality. The results of testing at a particular dose may be either:

(a) less than 100% survival;
(b) 100% survival, but evident toxicity;
(c) 100% survival, but no evident toxicity.

The test method requires in some cases testing at higher or lower doses if not already tested at the relevant dose level. (Refer to the evaluation of the test method in Annex V of Directive 67/548/EEC.)

45 In the criteria below for very toxic, toxic and harmful, only the final test result is shown. The 2000 mg/kg dose should be used primarily to obtain information on the toxic effects of substances which are of low acute toxicity and which are not classified on the basis of acute toxicity.

Very toxic

46 Substances and preparations should be classified as very toxic, assigned the corresponding symbol 'T+' with the indication of danger 'very toxic' and the appropriate risk phrases in accordance with the following criteria:

Acute lethal effects

R28 *Very toxic if swallowed*

Acute toxicity results:

LD_{50} oral, rat:
≤ 25 mg/kg

less than 100% survival at 5 mg/kg oral, rat, by the fixed dose procedure.

R27 *Very toxic in contact with skin*

Acute toxicity results:

LD_{50} dermal, rat or rabbit:
≤ 50 mg/kg

R26 *Very toxic by inhalation*

Acute toxicity results:

LC_{50} inhalation, rat, for aerosols or particulates:
≤ 0.25 mg/litre/4hr

LC_{50} inhalation, rat, for gases and vapours:
≤ 0.5 mg/litre/4hr

Non-lethal irreversible effects after a single exposure

R39 *Danger of very serious irreversible effects*

Strong evidence that irreversible damage (other than the effects referred to in paragraphs 77 to 115) is likely to be caused by a single exposure by an appropriate route, generally in the above dose ranges (see also paragraphs 38 to 39).

To indicate the route of administration/exposure one of the following combinations of risk phrases shall be used: R39/26, R39/27, R39/28, R39/26/27, R39/26/28, R39/27/28, R39/26/27/28.

Toxic

47 Substances and preparations should be classified as toxic, assigned the corresponding symbol 'T' with the indication of danger 'toxic' and the appropriate risk phrases in accordance with the following criteria:

Acute lethal effects

R25 *Toxic if swallowed*

Acute toxicity results:

LD_{50} oral, rat:
$25 < LD_{50} \leq 200$ mg/kg

Discriminating dose, oral, rat, 5 mg/kg:
100% survival but evident toxicity.

R24 *Toxic in contact with skin*

Acute toxicity results:

LD_{50} dermal, rat or rabbit:
$50 < LD_{50} \leq 400$ mg/kg

R23 *Toxic by inhalation*

Acute toxicity results:

LC_{50} inhalation, rat, for aerosols or particulates:
$0.25 < LC_{50} \leq 1$ mg/litre/4hr

LC_{50} inhalation, rat, for gases and vapours:
$0.5 < LC_{50} \leq 2$ mg/litre/4hr

R39 *Danger of very serious irreversible effects*

Strong evidence that irreversible damage other than the effects referred to in paragraphs 77 to 115 is likely to be caused by a single exposure by an appropriate route, generally in the above dose ranges (see also paragraphs 38 to 39).

To indicate the route of administration/exposure one of the following combinations shall be used: R39/23, R39/24, R39/25, R39/23/24, R39/23/25, R39/24/25, R39/23/24/25.

Severe effects after repeated or prolonged exposure

R48 *Danger of serious damage to health by prolonged exposure*

Serious damage (clear functional disturbance or morphological change which has toxicological significance) is likely to be caused by repeated or prolonged exposure by an appropriate route. Substances and preparations are classified at least as Toxic with R48 when these effects are observed at levels of the order of:

oral, rat	$\leq$ 5 mg/kg (body weight)/day
dermal, rat or rabbit	$\leq$ 10 mg/kg (body weight)/day
inhalation, rat	$\leq$ 0.025 mg/l, 6hr/day

These guide values can apply directly when severe lesions have been observed in a subchronic (90 days) toxicity test. When interpreting the results of a sub-acute (28 days) toxicity test, these figures should be increased approximately three fold. If a chronic (2 years) toxicity test is available it should be evaluated on a case-by-case basis. If results of studies of more than one duration are available, then those from the study of the longest duration should normally be used. Further information on the use of R48 is given in paragraphs 50 to 54.

To indicate the route of administration/exposure one of the following combinations shall be used: R48/23, R48/24, R48/25, R48/23/24, R48/23/25, R48/24/25, R48/23/24/25.

Harmful

48 Substances and preparations should be classified as harmful, assigned the corresponding symbol 'Xn' with the indication of danger 'harmful' and the appropriate risk phrases in accordance with the following criteria:

Acute lethal effects

R22 *Harmful if swallowed*

Acute toxicity results:

LD_{50} oral, rat:
$200 < LD_{50} \leq 2000$ mg/kg

Discriminating dose, oral, rat, 50 mg/kg:
100% survival but evident toxicity

less than 100% survival at 500 mg/kg oral, rat by the fixed dose procedure. Refer to the evaluation of the test method in Annex V of Directive 67/548/EEC.

R21 *Harmful in contact with skin*

Acute toxicity results:

LD_{50} dermal, rat or rabbit:
$400 < LD_{50} \leq 2000$ mg/kg

R20 *Harmful by inhalation*

Acute toxicity results:

LC_{50} inhalation, rat for aerosols or particulates:
$1 < LC_{50} \leq 5$ mg/litre/4hr

LC_{50} inhalation, rat for gases or vapours:
$2 < LC_{50} \leq 20$ mg/litre/4hr

Aspiration hazard

R65 *Harmful: may cause lung damage if swallowed*

Liquid substances and preparations presenting an aspiration hazard in humans because of their low viscosity:

(a) For substances and preparations containing aliphatic alicyclic and aromatic hydrocarbons in a total concentration equal to or greater than 10% and having:

   (i) a flow time of less than 30 sec in a 3 mm ISO cup according to EN 535; or

   (ii) a kinematic viscosity measured by a calibrated glass capillary viscometer in accordance with ISO 3104/3105 of less than 7×10^{-6} m^2/sec at 40°C; or

   (iii) a kinematic viscosity derived from measurements of rotational viscometry in accordance with ISO 3219 of less than 7×10^{-6} m^2/sec at 40°C.

Note that substances and preparations meeting these criteria need not be classified if they have a mean surface tension greater than 25 mN/m at 40°C.

(b) For other substances and preparations, not subject to the above criteria, based on practical experience in humans.

Non-lethal irreversible effects after a single exposure

R40 *Possible risk of irreversible effects*

Strong evidence that irreversible damage other than effects referred to in paragraphs 77 to 115 is likely to be caused by a single exposure by an appropriate route, generally in the above dose ranges (see also paragraphs 38 to 39).

To indicate route of administration/exposure one of the following combinations shall be used: R40/20, R40/21, R40/22, R40/20/21, R40/20/22, R40/21/22, R40/20/21/22.

Severe effects after repeated or prolonged exposure

R48 *Danger of serious damage to health by prolonged exposure*

Serious damage (clear functional disturbance or morphological change which has toxicological significance) is likely to be caused by repeated or prolonged exposure by an appropriate route.

Substances and preparations are classified at least as 'harmful' with R48 when these effects are observed at levels of the order of:

oral, rat	≤ 50 mg/kg (body weight)/day
dermal, rat or rabbit	≤ 100 mg/kg (body weight)/day
inhalation, rat	≤ 0.25 mg/litre, 6hr/day

See also the explanation under R48 in paragraph 47. Further information on the use of R48 is given in paragraphs 50 to 54.

To indicate route of administration/exposure one of the following combinations shall be used: R48/20, R48/21, R48/22, R48/20/21, R48/20/22, R48/21/22, R48/20/21/22.

Comments regarding very volatile substances

49 For certain substances with a high saturated vapour concentration, evidence may be available to indicate effects that give cause for concern. Such substances may not be classified under the criteria for health effects in this Guide. However, where there is appropriate evidence that such substances may present a risk in normal handling and use, then classification as 'harmful' on a case by case basis with an appropriate phrase may be necessary.

NB Such substances will be classified in the Approved Supply List with appropriate concentration limits.

Criteria for use of R48

50 Use of this risk phrase refers to the specific range of biological effects within the terms described below. For application of this risk phrase serious damage to health is to be considered to include death, clear functional disturbance or morphological changes which are toxicologically significant. It is particularly important when these changes are irreversible. It is also important to consider not only specific severe changes in a single organ or biological system but also generalised changes of a less severe nature involving several organs, or severe changes in general health status.

51 When assessing whether there is evidence for these types of effects, reference should be made to the guidelines in paragraphs 52 to 54.

Evidence indicating that R48 should be applied

52 The evidence includes:

(a) substance-related deaths;

(b) major functional changes in:

- (i) the central or peripheral nervous systems, including sight, hearing and the sense of smell, assessed by clinical observations or other appropriate methods (eg electrophysiology);
- (ii) other organ systems (for example the lung);

(c) any consistent changes in clinical biochemistry, haematology or urinalysis parameters which indicate severe organ dysfunction. Haematological disturbances are considered to be particularly important if the evidence suggests that they are due to decreased bone marrow production of blood cells;

(d) severe organ damage noted in microscopic examination following autopsy:

- (i) widespread or severe necrosis, fibrosis or granuloma formation in vital organs with regenerative capacity (eg liver);
- (ii) severe morphological changes that are potentially reversible but are clear evidence of marked organ dysfunction (eg severe fatty change in the liver, severe acute tubular nephrosis in the kidney, ulcerative gastritis);
- (iii) evidence of appreciable cell death in vital organs incapable of regeneration (eg fibrosis of the myocardium or dying back

of a nerve) or in stem cell populations (eg aplasia or hypoplasia of the bone marrow).

53 The above evidence will most usually be obtained from animal experiments. When considering data derived from practical experience, special attention should be given to exposure levels.

Evidence indicating that R48 should not be applied

54 The use of this risk phrase is restricted to 'serious damage to health by prolonged exposure'. A number of substance-related effects may be observed in both humans and animals that would not justify the use of R48. These effects are relevant when attempting to determine a no-effect level for a chemical substance. Examples of well-documented changes which would not normally justify classification with R48, irrespective of their statistical significance, include:

(a) clinical observations or changes in body weight gain, food consumption or water intake, which may have some toxicological importance but which do not, by themselves, indicate 'serious damage';

(b) small changes in clinical biochemistry, haematology or urinalysis parameters which are of doubtful or minimal toxicological importance;

(c) changes in organ weights with no evidence of organ dysfunction;

(d) adaptive responses (eg macrophage migration in the lung, liver hypertrophy and enzyme induction, hyperplastic responses to irritants). Local effects on the skin produced by repeated dermal application of a substance which are more appropriately classified with R38 'Irritating to skin';

(e) where a species-specific mechanism of toxicity (eg by specific metabolic pathways) has been demonstrated.

Corrosive

55 A substance or a preparation is considered to be corrosive if, when it is applied to healthy intact animal skin, it produces full thickness destruction of skin tissue on at least one animal during the test for skin irritation cited in Annex V of Directive 67/548/EEC or during an equivalent method or if the results can be predicted, for example from strong acid or alkaline reactions (demonstrated pH of 2 or less or 11.5 or greater. Alkaline or acidic reserve should also be taken into account). Classification can be based on the results of validated *in vitro* tests.

56 Substances or preparations should be classified as corrosive, assigned the corresponding symbol 'C' with the indication of danger 'corrosive' and the appropriate risk phrase in accordance with the following criteria:

R35 *Causes severe burns*

If, when applied to healthy intact animal skin, full thickness destruction of skin tissue occurs as a result of up to 3 minutes exposure, or if this result can be predicted.

R34 *Causes burns*

If, when applied to healthy intact animal skin, full thickness destruction of skin tissue occurs as a result of up to 4 hours exposure, or if this result can be predicted.

Organic hydroperoxides, except where evidence to the contrary is available.

Irritant

57 Substances and preparations should be classified as irritant, assigned the corresponding symbol 'Xi' with the indication of danger 'irritant' and the appropriate risk phrases in accordance with the following criteria:

R38 *Irritating to skin*

If they cause significant inflammation of the skin which persists for at least 24 hours after an exposure period of up to 4 hours determined on the rabbit according to the cutaneous irritation test method cited in Annex V of Directive 67/548/EEC.

Inflammation of the skin is significant if:

(a) the mean value of the scores for either erythema and eschar formation or oedema formation, calculated over all animals tested, is two or more; or

(b) in the case where the Annex V test has been completed using three animals, either erythema and eschar formation or oedema formation equivalent to a mean value of two or more calculated for each animal separately has been observed in two or more animals.

In both cases, all scores at each of the reading times (24, 48, 72 hours) for an effect should be used in calculating the respective mean values.

(c) it persists in at least two animals at the end of the observation time. Particular effects, eg hyperplasia, scaling, discoloration, fissures, scabs and alopecia should be taken into account.

Substances and preparations which cause significant inflammation of the skin, based on practical observations in humans.

Organic peroxides, except where evidence to the contrary is available.

Irritation due to defatting properties of a substance

58 When test results or practical experience show irritation in accordance with the above criteria, R-phrases should be used. However, S-phrases (eg S24, S28, S37) should be used when there are reasons to suspect that the defatting properties of the substance may cause irritation in man even though the above criteria are not met, or if an inappropriate test has been used.

R36 *Irritating to eyes*

If when applied to the eye of the animal, significant ocular lesions occur within 72 hours after exposure and persist for at least 24 hours.

Ocular lesions are significant if they correspond to the following mean values determined on the rabbit according to the eye irritation test described in Annex V of Directive 67/548/EEC.

Either:

(a) the mean value of the scores for each type of lesion, calculated over all animals tested, is one of the following:

cornea opacity	2 ≤ score < 3
iris lesion	1 ≤ score ≤ 1.5
redness of conjunctiva	≥ 2.5
oedema of conjunctiva (chemosis)	≥ 2;

or

(b) in the case where the Annex V test has been completed using three animals, a lesion equivalent to one of the mean values quoted below, but calculated for each animal separately, has been observed in two or more animals:

cornea opacity	2 ≤ value < 3
iris lesion	1 ≤ value < 2
redness of conjunctiva	≥ 2.5
oedema of conjunctiva (chemosis)	≥ 2

In both cases all scores at each of the reading times (24, 48, 72 hours) for an effect should be used in calculating the respective mean values.

Substances or preparations which cause significant ocular lesions, based on practical experience in humans.

Organic peroxides except where evidence to the contrary is available.

R41 *Risk of serious damage to eyes*

If when applied to the eye of the animal severe ocular lesions are caused which occur within 72 hours after exposure and which are present 24 hours or more after instillation of the test material.

Ocular lesions are severe if the means of the scores calculated over all the animals tested have any of the values:

cornea opacity	≥ 3
iris lesion	> 1.5

The same shall be the case where the test has been completed using three animals if these lesions, on two or more animals, have any of the values:

cornea opacity	≥ 3
iris lesion	= 2

In both cases all scores at each of the reading times (24, 48 and 72 hours) for an effect should be used in calculating the respective mean values.

Ocular lesions are also severe:

(a) when they are still present at the end of the observation time;

(b) if the substance or preparation causes irreversible coloration of the eyes.

Substances and preparations which cause severe ocular lesions, based on practical experience in humans.

Note: When a substance or preparation is classified as corrosive and assigned R34 or R35, the risk of severe damage to eyes is considered implicit and R41 is not included in the label. However, in the case of preparations, when calculating the sum of quotients by the formulae in Schedule 3 of the CHIP Regulations, substances classified as corrosive shall be considered as if R41 had been assigned.

Respiratory system irritation

R37 *Irritating to respiratory system*

For substances and preparations which cause serious irritation to the respiratory system, normally based on:

(a) practical observation in humans;

(b) positive results from appropriate animal tests.

Comments regarding the use of R37

59 In interpreting practical observations in humans, care should be taken to distinguish between effects which lead to classification with R48 (see paragraphs 50 to 54) from those leading to classification with R37. Conditions normally leading to classification with R37 are reversible and usually limited to the upper airways.

60 Positive results from appropriate animal tests may include data obtained in a general toxicity test, including histopathological data from the respiratory system. Data from the measurement of experimental bradypnea may also be used to assess airway irritation.

Sensitising

Sensitisation by inhalation

61 Substances and preparations should be classified as sensitising and assigned the symbol 'Xn', with the indication of danger 'harmful', and the risk phrase R42 in accordance with the following criteria:

R42 *May cause sensitisation by inhalation*

If there is evidence that the substance or preparation can induce specific respiratory hypersensitivity.

Where there are positive results from appropriate animal tests.

If the substance is an isocyanate, unless there is evidence that the substance does not cause respiratory hypersensitivity.

Comments regarding the use of R42

Human evidence

62 Evidence that the substance can induce specific respiratory hypersensitivity will normally be based on human experience. In this context hypersensitivity is normally seen as asthma, but other hypersensitivity reactions such as rhinitis and alveolitis are also considered. The condition will have the clinical character of an allergic reaction. However, immunological mechanisms do not have to be demonstrated.

63 When considering the evidence from human exposure, it is necessary for a decision on classification to take into account, in addition to the evidence from the cases:

(a) the size of the population exposed;

(b) the extent of exposure.

64 The evidence referred to above could be clinical history and data from appropriate lung function tests related to exposure to the substance, confirmed by other supportive evidence which may include:

(a) a chemical structure related to substances known to cause respiratory hypersensitivity;

(b) *in vivo* immunological test (eg skin prick test);

(c) *in vitro* immunological test (eg serological analysis);

(d) studies that may indicate other specific but non-immunological mechanisms of action, eg repeated low-level irritation, pharmacologically mediated effects;

(e) data from a positive bronchial challenge test with the substance conducted according to accepted guidelines for the determination of a specific hypersensitivity reaction.

65 Clinical history should include both medical and occupational history to determine a relationship between exposure to a specific substance and development of respiratory hypersensitivity. Relevant information includes aggravating factors both in the home and workplace, the onset and progress of the disease, family history and medical history of the patient in question. The medical history should also include a note of other allergic or airway disorders from childhood, and smoking history.

66 The results of positive bronchial challenge tests are considered to provide sufficient evidence for classification on their own. It is however recognised that in practice many of the examinations listed above will already have been carried out.

67 Substances that elicit symptoms of asthma by irritation only in people with bronchial hyperreactivity should not be assigned R42.

Animal studies

68 Data from tests which may be indicative of the potential of a substance to cause sensitisation by inhalation in humans may include:

(a) IgE measurements (eg in mice);

(b) specific pulmonary responses in guinea pigs.

Sensitisation by skin contact

69 Substances and preparations should be classified as sensitising and assigned the symbol 'Xi', with the indication of danger 'irritant' and the appropriate risk phrase in accordance with the following criteria:

R43 *May cause sensitisation by skin contact*

If practical experience shows the substances and preparations to be capable of inducing a sensitisation reaction in a substantial number of people.

Where there are positive results from an appropriate animal test.

Comments regarding the use of R43

Human evidence

70 The following evidence (practical experience) is sufficient to classify a substance with R43:

(a) positive data from appropriate patch testing, normally in more than one dermatological clinic; or

(b) epidemiological studies showing allergic contact dermatitis caused by the substance. Situations in which a high proportion of those exposed exhibit characteristic symptoms are to be looked at with special concern, even if the number of cases is small; or

(c) positive data from experimental studies in man (see also paragraph 37).

71 The following is sufficient to classify a substance with R43 when there is supportive evidence:

(a) isolated episodes of allergic contact dermatitis; or

(b) epidemiological studies where chance, bias or confounders have not been ruled out fully with reasonable confidence.

72 Supportive evidence may include:

(a) data from animal tests performed according to existing guidelines, with a result that does not meet the criteria given in the section on animal studies but is sufficiently close to the limit to be considered significant; or

(b) data from non-standard methods; or

(c) appropriate structure-activity relationships.

Animal studies

73 Positive results from appropriate animal tests are:

(a) in the case of the adjuvant type test method for skin sensitisation detailed in Annex V of Directive 67/548/EEC;* or

(b) in the case of other adjuvant-type test methods, a response of at least 30% of the animals is considered as positive; and

(c) for any other test method a response of at least 15% of the animals is considered positive.

* Annex V to this Directive has been adopted in the UK as an Approved Code of Practice under section 16(1) of the Health and Safety at Work Act 1974. The Notice of Approval is reproduced at Appendix 2 to this Guide.

Immunological contact urticaria

74 Some substances which meet the criteria for R42 may in addition cause immunological contact urticaria. In these cases, information concerning contact urticaria should be included by the use of appropriate S-phrases, usually S24 and S36/37, and in the safety data sheet.

75 For substances which produce signs of immunological contact urticaria which do not fulfil the criteria for R42, consideration should be given to classification with R43.

76 There is no recognised animal model available to identify substances which cause immunological contact urticaria. Therefore, classification will normally be based on human evidence which will be similar to that for skin sensitisation (R43).

Note: that if the symbol 'Xn' and the indication of danger 'harmful' are assigned, the symbol 'Xi' and the indication of danger 'irritant' are optional.

Carcinogenic, mutagenic and toxic to reproduction

77 Substances that may be carcinogenic, mutagenic or toxic to reproduction should be classified in accordance with the criteria below (see also paragraphs 14 to 17). Preparations that contain one or more substances classified as carcinogenic, mutagenic or toxic to reproduction should be classified using the conventional method (see paragraph 39).

Carcinogenic substances

78 For the purpose of classification and labelling, and having regard to the current state of knowledge, such substances are divided into three categories.

Category 1

79 These are substances known to be carcinogenic to man. There is sufficient evidence to establish a causal association between human exposure to a substance and the development of cancer.

Category 2

80 These are substances which should be regarded as if they are carcinogenic to man. There is sufficient evidence to provide a strong presumption that human exposure to a substance may result in the development of cancer, generally on the basis of:

(a) appropriate long-term animal studies;

(b) other relevant information.

Category 3

81 These are substances which cause concern for man owing to possible carcinogenic effects but in respect of which the available information is not adequate for making a satisfactory assessment. There is some evidence from appropriate animal studies, but this is insufficient to place the substance in Category 2.

82 The following symbols and specific risk phrases apply:

Categories 1 and 2

T; R45 *May cause cancer*

83 However, for substances and preparations which present a carcinogenic risk only when inhaled, for example, as dust, vapour or fumes, and for which other routes of exposure such as swallowing or contact with skin do not present any carcinogenic risk, the following symbol and specific risk phrase should be used:

T; R49 *May cause cancer by inhalation*

Category 3

Xn; R40 *Possible risk of irreversible effects*

Criteria for the categorisation of carcinogenic substances

84 The placing of a substance into Category 1 is done on the basis of epidemiological data; placing into Categories 2 and 3 is based primarily on animal experiments.

85 For classification as a Category 2 carcinogen, either positive results in two animal species should be available or clear positive evidence in one species, together with supporting evidence such as genotoxicity data, metabolic or biochemical studies, induction of benign tumours, structural relationship with other known carcinogens, or data from epidemiological studies suggesting an association.

86 Category 3 actually comprises two sub-categories:

(a) substances which are well investigated but for which the evidence of a tumour-inducing effect is insufficient for classification in Category 2. Additional experiments would not be expected to yield further relevant information with respect to classification;

(b) substances which are insufficiently investigated. The available data is inadequate, but raises concern for man. This classification is provisional; further experiments are necessary before a final decision can be made.

87 Relevant arguments to distinguish between Categories 2 and 3 are listed below. Their effect is to reduce the significance of experimental tumour induction for possible human exposure as, especially in combination, they lead in most cases to classification in Category 3, even though tumours have been induced in animals:

(a) carcinogenic effects only at very high dose levels exceeding the 'maximal tolerated dose'. The maximal tolerated dose is characterised by toxic effects which, although not yet reducing lifespan, are associated with physical changes such as about 10% retardation in weight gain;

(b) appearance of tumours, especially at high dose levels, only in particular organs of certain species known to be susceptible to a high spontaneous tumour formation;

(c) appearance of tumours only at the site of application, in very sensitive test systems (eg, i.p. or s.c. application of certain locally active compounds), if the particular target is not relevant to man;

(d) lack of genotoxicity in short-term tests *in vivo* and *in vitro*;

(e) existence of a secondary mechanism of action with the implication of a practical threshold above a certain dose level (eg hormonal effects on target organs or on mechanisms of physiological regulation, chronic stimulation of cell proliferation);

(f) existence of a species-specific mechanism of tumour formation (eg by specific metabolic pathways) irrelevant for man.

88 Relevant arguments to distinguish between Category 3 and no classification are those which exclude a concern for man:

(a) a substance should not be classified in any of the categories if the mechanism of experimental tumour formation is clearly identified, with good evidence that this process cannot be extrapolated to man;

(b) if the only available tumour data are liver tumours in certain sensitive strains of mice, without any other supplementary evidence, the substance may not be classified in any of the categories;

(c) particular attention should be paid to cases where the only available tumour data are the occurrence of neoplasms at sites and in strains where they are well known to occur spontaneously with a high incidence.

Mutagenic substances

89 For the purposes of classification and labelling, and having regard to the current state of knowledge, such substances are divided into three categories.

Category 1

90 These are substances known to be mutagenic to man. There is sufficient evidence to establish a causal association between human exposure to a substance and heritable genetic damage.

Category 2

91 These are substances which should be regarded as if they are mutagenic to man. There is sufficient evidence to provide a strong presumption that human exposure to the substance may result in the development of heritable genetic damage, generally on the basis of:

(a) appropriate animal studies;

(b) other relevant information.

Category 3

92 These are substances which cause concern for man owing to possible mutagenic effects. There is evidence from appropriate mutagenicity studies, but this is insufficient to place the substance in Category 2.

93 The following symbols and specific risk phrases apply:

Category 1

T; R46 *May cause heritable genetic damage*

Category 2

T; R46 *May cause heritable genetic damage*

Category 3

Xn; R40 *Possible risk of irreversible effects*

Criteria for the categorisation of mutagenic substances

Definition of terms

94 A mutation is a permanent change in the amount or structure of the genetic material in an organism, resulting in a change of the phenotypic characteristics of the organism. The alterations may involve a single gene, a block of genes, or a whole chromosome. Effects involving single genes may be a consequence of effects on single DNA bases (point mutations) or of large changes, including deletions, within the gene. Effects on whole chromosomes may involve structural or numerical changes. A mutation in the germ cells in sexually reproducing organisms may be transmitted to the offspring. A mutagen is an agent that gives rise to an enhanced occurrence of mutations.

95 It should be noted that substances are classified as mutagens with specific reference to inherited genetic damage. However, the type of results leading to classification of chemicals in Category 3, 'induction of genetically relevant events in somatic cells', is generally also regarded as an alert for possible carcinogenic activity.

96 Method development for mutagenicity testing is an on-going process. For many new tests no standardised protocols and evaluation criteria are presently available. To evaluate the mutagenicity data, the quality of the test performance and the degree of validation of the test method have to be considered.

Category 1

97 To place a substance in Category 1, positive evidence from human mutation epidemiology studies will be needed. Examples of such substances are not known to date. It is recognised that it is extremely difficult to obtain reliable information from studies on the incidence of mutations in human populations, or on possible increases in their frequencies.

Category 2

98 To place a substance in Category 2, positive results are needed from assays showing (a) mutagenic effects, or (b) other cellular interactions relevant to mutagenicity, in germ cells of mammals *in vivo*, or (c) mutagenic effects in somatic cells of mammals *in vivo* in combination with clear evidence that the substance or a relevant metabolite reaches the germ cells. At present the following methods (2a, 2b and 2c) are appropriate:

(2a) *In vivo* germ cell mutagenicity assays:

- specific locus mutation test;
- heritable translocation test;
- dominant lethal mutation test.

These assays actually demonstrate the appearance of affected progeny or a defect in the developing embryo.

(2b) *In vivo* assays showing relevant interaction with germ cells (usually DNA):

- assays for chromosomal abnormalities, as detected by cytogenetic analysis, including aneuploidy, caused by malsegregation of chromosomes;

- test for sister chromatid exchanges (SCEs);

- test for unscheduled DNA synthesis (UDS);

- assay of (covalent) binding of mutagen to germ cell DNA;

- assaying other kinds of DNA damage.

These assays provide evidence of a more or less indirect nature. Positive results in these assays would normally be supported by positive results from *in vivo* somatic cell mutagenicity assays, in mammals or in man (see under Category 3, preferably methods as under 3a).

(2c) *In vivo* assays showing mutagenic effects in somatic cells of mammals (see under 3a), in combination with toxicokinetic methods, or other methodologies capable of demonstrating that the compound or a relevant metabolite reaches the germ cells.

For 2b and 2c, positive results from host-mediated assays or the demonstration of unequivocal effects *in vitro* assays can be considered as supporting evidence.

Category 3

99 To place a substance in Category 3, positive results are needed in assays showing (a) mutagenic effects or (b) other cellular interaction relevant to mutagenicity, in somatic cells in mammals *in vivo*. The latter especially would normally be supported by positive results from *in vitro* mutagenicity assays. For effects in somatic cells *in vivo* at present the following methods are appropriate:

(3a) *in vivo* somatic cell mutagenicity assays:

- bone marrow micronucleus test or metaphase analysis;

- metaphase analysis of peripheral lymphocytes;

- mouse coat colour spot test.

(3b) *in vivo* somatic cell DNA interaction assays:

- test for SCEs in somatic cells;

- test for UDS in somatic cells;

- assay for the (covalent) binding of mutagen to somatic cell DNA;

- assay for DNA damage, eg by alkaline elution, in somatic cells.

100 Substances showing positive results only in one or more *in vitro* mutagenicity assays should normally not be classified. Their further investigation using *in vivo* assays, however, is strongly indicated. In exceptional cases, eg for a substance showing pronounced responses in several *in vitro* assays, for which no relevant *in vivo* data are available, and which shows resemblance to known mutagens/carcinogens, classification in Category 3 could be considered.

Substances toxic to reproduction

101 For the purposes of classification and labelling and having regard to the present state of knowledge, such substances are divided into three categories:

Category 1

(a) Substances known to impair fertility in humans. There is sufficient evidence to establish a causal relationship between human exposure to the substance and impaired fertility.

(b) Substances known to cause developmental toxicity in humans. There is sufficient evidence to establish a causal relationship between human exposure to the substance and subsequent development toxic effects in the progeny.

Category 2

(a) Substances which should be regarded as if they impair fertility in humans. There is sufficient evidence to provide a strong presumption that human exposure to the substance may result in impaired fertility on the basis of:

  (i) clear evidence in animal studies of impaired fertility in the absence of toxic effects, or evidence of impaired fertility occurring at around the same dose levels as other toxic effects but which is not a secondary non-specific consequence of the other toxic effects;

  (ii) other relevant information.

(b) Substances which should be regarded as if they cause developmental toxicity to humans. There is sufficient evidence to provide a strong presumption that human exposure to the substance may result in developmental toxicity, generally on the basis of:

  (i) clear results in appropriate animal studies where effects have been observed in the absence of signs of marked material toxicity, or at around the same dose levels as other toxic effects but which are not a secondary non-specific consequence of the other toxic effects;

  (ii) other relevant information.

Category 3

(a) Substances which cause concern for human fertility, generally on the basis of:

  (i) results in appropriate animal studies which provide sufficient evidence to cause a strong suspicion of impaired fertility in the absence of toxic effects, or evidence of impaired fertility occurring at around the same dose levels as other toxic effects, but which is not a secondary non-specific consequence of the other toxic effects, but where the evidence is insufficient to place the substance in Category 2;

  (ii) other relevant information.

(b) Substances which cause concern for humans owing to possible developmental toxic effects, generally on the basis of:

(i) results in appropriate animal studies which provide sufficient evidence to cause a strong suspicion of developmental toxicity in the absence of signs of marked maternal toxicity, or at around the same dose levels as other toxic effects but which are not a secondary non-specific consequence of the other toxic effects, but where the evidence is insufficient to place the substance in Category 2;

(ii) other relevant information.

102 The following symbols and specific risk phrases apply:

Category 1

For substances that impair fertility in humans:

T; R60 *May impair fertility*

For substances that cause developmental toxicity:

T; R61 *May cause harm to the unborn child*

Category 2

For substances that should be regarded as if they impair fertility in humans:

T; R60 *May impair fertility*

For substances that should be regarded as if they cause developmental toxicity in humans:

T; R61 *May cause harm to the unborn child*

Category 3

For substances which cause concern for human fertility:

Xn; R62 *Possible risk of impaired fertility*

For substances which cause concern for humans owing to possible developmental toxic effects:

Xn; R63 *Possible risk of harm to the unborn child*

Comments regarding the categorisation of substances toxic to reproduction

103 Reproductive toxicity includes impairment of male and female reproductive functions or capacity and the induction of non-inheritable harmful effects on the progeny. This may be classified under two main headings (a) Effects on male or female fertility and (b) Developmental toxicity.

(a) ***Effects on male or female fertility*** includes adverse effects on libido, sexual behaviour, any aspect of spermatogenesis or oogenesis, or on hormonal activity or physiological response which would interfere with the capacity to fertilise, fertilisation itself or the development of the fertilised ovum up to and including implantation.

(b) ***Developmental toxicity*** is taken in its widest sense to include any effect interfering with normal development, both before and after birth. It includes effects induced or manifested prenatally as well as those manifested postnatally. This includes embrytoxic/fetotoxic effects such as reduced body weight, growth and developmental retardation, organ toxicity, death, abortion, structural defects (teratogenic effects), functional defects, peri-postnatal defects, and impaired postnatal mental or physical development up to and including normal pubertal development.

104 Classification of chemicals as 'toxic to reproduction' is intended to be used for chemicals which have an intrinsic or specific property to produce such toxic effects. Chemicals should not be classified as toxic to reproduction where such effects are solely produced as a non-specific secondary consequence of other toxic effects. Chemicals of most concern are those which are toxic to reproduction at exposure levels which do not produce other signs of toxicity.

105 The placing of a compound in Category 1 for effects on fertility and/or developmental toxicity is done on the basis of epidemiological data. Placing into Categories 2 or 3 is done primarily on the basis of animal data. Data from *in vitro* studies, or studies on avian eggs, are regarded as 'supportive evidence' and would only exceptionally lead to classification in the absence of *in vivo* data.

106 In common with most other types of toxic effect, substances demonstrating reproductive toxicity will be expected to have a threshold below which adverse effects would not be demonstrated. Even when clear effects have been demonstrated in animal studies, the relevance for humans may be doubtful because of the doses administered, for example, where effects have been demonstrated only at high doses, or where marked toxicokinetic differences exist, or the route of administration is inappropriate. For these or similar reasons it may be that classification in Category 3, or even no classification, will be warranted.

107 Annex V of Directive 67/548/EEC specifies a limit test in the case of substances of low toxicity. If a dose level of at least 1000 mg/kg orally produces no evidence of effects toxic to reproduction, studies at other dose levels may not be considered necessary. If data are available from studies carried out with doses higher than the above limit dose, these data must be evaluated together with other relevant data. Under normal circumstances it is considered that effects seen only at doses in excess of the limit dose would not necessarily lead to classification as toxic to reproduction.

Effects on fertility

108 For the classification of a substance into Category 2 for impaired fertility, there should normally be clear evidence in one animal species, with supporting evidence on mechanism of action or site of action, or chemical relationship to other known anti-fertility agents or other information from humans which would lead to the conclusion that effects would be likely to be seen in humans. Where there are studies in only one species without other relevant supporting evidence then classification in Category 3 may be appropriate.

109 Since impaired fertility may occur as a non-specific accompaniment to severe generalised toxicity or where there is severe inanition, classification into Category 2 should only be made where there is evidence that there is some degree of specificity of toxicity for the reproductive system. If it was demonstrated that impaired fertility in animal studies was due to failure to mate then, for classification into Category 2, it would normally be necessary to have evidence on the mechanism of action to interpret whether any adverse effect such as alteration in pattern of hormonal release would be likely to occur in humans.

Developmental toxicity

110 For classification into Category 2 there should be clear evidence of adverse effects in well-conducted studies in one or more species. Since adverse effects in pregnancy or postnatally may result as a secondary consequence of maternal toxicity, reduced food or water intake, maternal stress, lack of maternal care, specific dietary deficiencies, poor animal husbandry, intercurrent infections, and so on, it is important that the effects observed should occur in well-conducted studies and at dose levels which are not associated with marked maternal toxicity. The route of exposure is also important. In particular, the injection of irritant material intraperitoneally may result in local damage to the uterus and its contents, and the results of such studies must be interpreted with caution and on their own would not normally lead to classification.

111 Classification into Category 3 is based on similar criteria as for Category 2 but may be used where the experimental design has deficiencies which make the conclusions less convincing, or where the possibility that the effects may have been due to non-specific influences such as generalised toxicity cannot be excluded.

112 In general, classification in Category 3 or no category would be assigned on an *ad hoc* basis where the only effects recorded are small changes in the incidences of spontaneous defects, small changes in the proportions of common variants such as are observed in skeletal examinations, or small differences in postnatal developmental assessments.

Effects during lactation

113 Substances which are classified as toxic to reproduction and which also cause concern due to their effects on lactation should in addition be labelled with R64 (see criteria in paragraph 119). For the purpose of classification, toxic effects on offspring resulting *only* from exposure via the breast milk, or toxic effects resulting from *direct* exposure of children will not be regarded as 'toxic to reproduction', unless such effects result in impaired development of the offspring. Substances which are not classified as toxic to reproduction but which cause concern due to toxicity when transferred to the baby during the period of lactation should be labelled with R64. This R-phrase may also be appropriate for substances which affect the quantity or quality of the milk.

114 R64 would normally be assigned on the basis of:

(a) toxicokinetic studies that would indicate the likelihood that the substance would be present in potentially toxic levels in breast milk; and/or

(b) on the basis of results of one or two generation studies in animals which indicates the presence of adverse effects on the offspring due to transfer in the milk; and/or

(c) on the basis of evidence in humans indicating a risk to babies during the lactation period.

115 Substances which are known to accumulate in the body and which subsequently may be released into milk during lactation may be labelled with R33 and R64.

Harmonised classification and labelling of carcinogens, mutagens and substances toxic for reproduction

116 If a manufacturer or his representative has information available indicating that a substance should be classified and labelled in accordance with the criteria in paragraphs 77 to 115, the substance should be labelled

accordingly. This label remains valid until an agreed entry is included in the Approved Supply List.

117 The manufacturer or his representative should also send to the Health and Safety Executive a document summarising the information on which the classification and label was based, unless such information has already been submitted to an authority nominated for that purpose in another member state in which the substance has been supplied. The summary document should include a bibliography containing all relevant references, including any relevant unpublished data.

118 The Health and Safety Executive will forward to the European Commission summary documents received. The European Commission will, in turn, forward the information to nominated authorities in other member states prior to discussion in an EC Working Group of National Experts on the Classification and Labelling of Dangerous Substances.

Other health effects

119 Additional risk phrases should be assigned to substances and preparations classified by virtue of paragraphs 26 to 118 and paragraphs 121 to 133.

R29 *Contact with water liberates toxic gas*

For substances and preparations which in contact with water or damp air, evolve very toxic/toxic gases in potentially dangerous amounts, eg aluminium phosphide, phosphorus pentasulphide.

R31 *Contact with acids liberates toxic gas*

For substances and preparations which react with acids to evolve toxic gases in dangerous amounts, eg sodium hypochlorite, barium polysulphide. For substances used by members of the general public, the use of S50 (*Do not mix with . . .* (to be specified by the manufacturer)) would be more suitable.

R32 *Contact with acids liberates very toxic gas*

For substances and preparations which react with acids to evolve very toxic gases in dangerous amounts, eg salts of hydrogen cyanide, sodium azide. For substances used by members of the general public, the use of S50 (*do not mix with . . .* (to be specified by the manufacturer)) would be more suitable.

R33 *Danger of cumulative effects*

For substances and preparations when accumulation in the human body is likely and may cause some concern which, however, is not sufficient to justify the use of R48.

R64 *May cause harm to breast-fed babies*

For substances and preparations which are absorbed by women and may interfere with lactation or which may be present (including metabolites) in breast milk in amounts sufficient to cause concern for the health of a breast-fed child.

For comments on the use of this R-phrase (and in some cases R 33) see paragraphs 103 to 115.

120 For other risk phrases see paragraph 34.

Classification on the basis of environmental effects

Criteria for classification, indication of danger and choice of risk phrases

121 The primary objective of classifying substances dangerous for the environment is to alert the user to the hazards these substances present to ecosystems. Although the present criteria refer largely to aquatic ecosystems it is recognised that certain substances may simultaneously or alternatively affect other ecosystems whose constituents may range from soil microflora and microfauna to primates.

122 The criteria set out in paragraphs 124 to 133 follow directly from the test methods set out in Annex V of Directive 67/548/EEC in so far as they are mentioned. The test methods required for the technical dossier as set out in Schedule 1 of the Notification of New Substances Regulations 1993 (NONS) are limited and the information derived from them may be insufficient for an appropriate classification. Classification may require additional data derived from Level 1 in Schedule 5 of the NONS Regulations or other equivalent studies. Furthermore, classified substances may be subject to review in the light of other new data.

123 For the purposes of classification and labelling and having regard to the current state of knowledge, such substances are divided into two groups according to their acute and/or long-term effects in aquatic systems or their acute and/or long-term effects in non-aquatic systems.

Aquatic environment

124 Substances should be classified as dangerous for the environment, assigned the corresponding symbol 'N' with the indication of danger 'dangerous for the environment' and the appropriate risk phrases in accordance with the following criteria:

R50 *Very toxic to aquatic organisms*

and

R53 *May cause long-term adverse effects in the aquatic environment*

Acute toxicity:

96 hr LC_{50} (for fish):
≤ 1 mg/l

or 48 hr EC_{50} (for daphnia):
≤ 1 mg/l

or 72 hr IC_{50} (for algae):
≤ 1 mg/l

and the substance is not readily degradable;

or the log Pow (log octanol/water partition coefficient) ≥ 3.0 (unless the experimentally determined bioconcentration factor (BCF) ≤ 100)

R50 *Very toxic to aquatic organisms*

Acute toxicity:

96 hr LC_{50} (for fish):
≤ 1 mg/l

or 48 hr EC_{50} (for daphnia):
≤ 1 mg/l

or 72 hr IC_{50} (for algae):
≤ 1 mg/l

R51 *Toxic to aquatic organisms*

and

R53 *May cause long-term adverse effects in the aquatic environment*

Acute toxicity:

96 hr LC_{50} (for fish):
1 mg/l< $LC_{50} \leq$ 10mg/l

or 48 hr EC_{50} (for daphnia):
1 mg/l< $EC_{50} \leq$ 10 mg/l

or 72 hr IC_{50} (for algae):
1 mg/l< $IC_{50} \leq$ 10 mg/l

and the substance is not readily degradable;

or the log Pow $\geq$ 3.0 (unless the experimentally determined BCF $\leq$ 100)

125 Substances should be classified as dangerous for the environment and assigned the appropriate risk phrases in accordance with the following criteria:

R52 *Harmful to aquatic organisms*

and

R53 *May cause long-term adverse effects in the aquatic environment*

Acute toxicity:

96 hr LC_{50} (for fish):
10 mg/l< $LC_{50} \leq$ 100mg/l

or 48 hr EC_{50} (for daphnia):
10 mg/l< $EC_{50} \leq$ 100mg/l

or 72 hr IC_{50} (for algae):
10 mg/l< $IC_{50} \leq$ 100mg/l

and the substance is not readily degradable.

126 These criteria apply unless there is sufficient additional scientific evidence concerning degradation and/or toxicity to provide adequate assurance that neither the substance nor its degradation products will constitute a

potential long-term and/or delayed danger to the aquatic environment. Such additional scientific evidence should normally be based on the studies required at Level 1 (Schedule 5 of the NONS Regulations) or studies of equivalent value, and could include:

(a) a proven potential to degrade rapidly in the aquatic environment;

(b) an absence of chronic toxicity effects at a concentration of 1.0 mg/litre, eg a no-observed effect concentration of greater than 1.0 mg/litre determined in a prolonged toxicity study with fish or daphnia.

127 Substances not falling under the criteria in paragraphs 124 and 125 but which on the basis of the available evidence concerning their toxicity may nevertheless present a danger to the structure and/or functioning of aquatic ecosystems should be assigned:

R52 *Harmful to aquatic organisms*

Substances not falling under the criteria listed in paragraphs 124 and 125, but which on the basis of the available evidence concerning their persistence, potential to accumulate and predicted, or observed, environmental fate and behaviour may nevertheless present a long-term and/or delayed danger to the structure and/or functioning of aquatic ecosystems should be assigned:

R53 *May cause long-term adverse effects in the aquatic environment*

For example, poorly water soluble substances, ie substances with a solubility of less than 1 mg/l will be covered by these criteria if:

(a) they are not readily degradable; and

(b) the log Pow $\geq$ 3.0 (unless the experimentally determined BCF $\leq$ 100).

128 The criteria in (a) and (b) above apply unless there is sufficient additional scientific evidence concerning degradation and/or toxicity sufficient to provide adequate assurance that neither the substance nor its degradation products will constitute a potential long-term and/or delayed danger to the aquatic environment. Such additional scientific evidence should normally be based on the studies required at Level 1 (Schedule 5 of NONS), or studies of equivalent value, and could include:

(a) a proven potential to degrade rapidly in the aquatic environment;

(b) an absence of chronic toxicity effects at the solubility limit, eg where the no-observed effect concentration determined in a prolonged toxicity study with fish or daphnia is greater than the solubility limit.

Comments on the determination of IC_{50} for algae and of degradability

129 Where it can be demonstrated in the case of highly coloured substances that algal growth is inhibited solely as a result of a reduction in light intensity, then the 72hr IC_{50} for algae should not be used as a basis for classification.

130 Substances are considered readily degradable if the following criteria hold true:

(a) if in 28-day biodegradation studies the following levels of degradation are achieved;

(i) in tests based upon dissolved organic carbon: 70%;

(ii) in tests based upon oxygen depletion or carbon dioxide generation: 60% of the theoretical maxima.

These levels of biodegradation must be achieved within 10 days of the start of degradation, which point is taken as the time when 10% of the substance has been degraded.

or

(b) if in those cases where only COD or BOD_5 data are available when the ratio of BOD_5/COD is greater than or equal to 0.5;

or

(c) if other convincing scientific evidence is available to demonstrate that the substance can be degraded (biotically and/or abiotically) in the aquatic environment to a level of > 70% within a 28-day period.

Non-aquatic environment

131 Substances should be classified as dangerous for the environment, assigned the corresponding symbol 'N' with the indication of danger 'dangerous for the environment' and at least one of the following risk phrases in accordance with the criteria set out in paragraphs 131 to 133:

R54 *Toxic to flora*

R55 *Toxic to fauna*

R56 *Toxic to soil organisms*

R57 *Toxic to bees*

R58 *May cause long-term adverse effects in the environment*

Substances which on the basis of the available evidence concerning their toxicity, persistence, potential to accumulate and predicted or observed environmental fate and behaviour may present a danger, immediate or long-term and/or delayed, to the structure and/or functioning of natural ecosystems other than those covered in paragraphs 119 to 125. Detailed criteria will be elaborated later.

132 Substances which on the basis of the available evidence concerning their properties and their predicted or observed environmental fate and behaviour may present a danger to the structure and/or the functioning of the stratospheric ozone layer should be assigned the symbol 'N' and the following phrase in accordance with the criteria set out below:

R59: *Dangerous for the ozone layer*

This includes the substances which are listed in Annex I Groups I, II, III, IV and V of Council Regulation (EEC) No 594/91 on substances that deplete the ozone layer (OJ No L 67 of 14 March 1991, p.1).

133 Substances not falling under the criteria in paragraph 131 which on the basis of the available evidence concerning their properties and their predicted or observed environmental fate and behaviour may present a danger to the structure and/or the functioning of the stratospheric ozone layer should be assigned the following risk phrase:

R59 *Dangerous to the ozone layer*

This includes the substances which are listed in Annex I Group VI to Council Regulation (EEC) No 594/91 on substances that deplete the ozone layer (OJ No L 67 of 14 March 1991, p.1).

Labelling

134 When a substance or preparation has been classified, the appropriate label is determined with reference to the requirements of regulations 9(2) and (3) of CHIP for substances and preparations respectively. This section explains how the label is determined and, in particular, gives guidance on how to select the appropriate risk and safety phrases.

135 For substances and preparations the risk phrases form part of the classification assigned in accordance with the criteria in paragraphs 21 to 35 for physico-chemical effects and paragraphs 36 to 120 for health effects. In addition, for substances, the classification includes any environmental risk phrases as set out in paragraphs 121 to 133. The prescribed safety phrases for substances and preparations are listed in the Appendix, together with the conditions that determine their application and use.

136 The label should contain the following information:

(a) name or names of the substances which will appear on the label;

(b) the name, address and telephone number of the person responsible for placing the substance or preparation on the market;

(c) the symbols and indication of danger;

(d) phrases indicating particular hazards (R-phrases);

(e) phrases indicating safety advice (S-phrases);

(f) for substances, the EEC number.

Note: For substances appearing in Annex I of Directive 67/548/EEC, the label also includes the words 'EEC label' or 'EC label'.

Choice of danger symbols

137 The design of the danger symbols and the wording of the indications of danger should comply with those laid down in Schedule 2 of the CHIP Regulations. The symbol should be printed in black on an orange-yellow background.

138 For substances appearing in the Approved Supply List the danger symbols and indications of danger should be those shown in the list.

139 For dangerous substances not yet appearing in the Approved Supply List and for preparations, the danger symbols and indications of danger shall be assigned according to the rules laid down in Part I of Schedule 6 of the CHIP Regulations.

Risk phrases

140 The wording of the risk phrases should comply with that laid down in Part III of Volume 1 of the Approved Supply List. The combined R-phrases should be used where applicable.

141 For ***substances***, the risk phrases that appear on the label should be selected according to the following criteria and priorities:

(a) In the case of health effects:

  (i) the risk phrases corresponding to the category of danger illustrated by the overriding symbol - see paragraph 4(1) of Part I of Schedule 6 of the CHIP Regulations. These phrases must appear on the label;

  (ii) the risk phrases corresponding to other categories of danger not illustrated by the overriding symbol;

(b) In the case of danger arising from physico-chemical properties:

  (i) the criteria described under (a) above are applicable, except that the risk phrases 'extremely flammable' or 'highly flammable' need not be indicated where they repeat the wording of the indication of danger used with a symbol;

(c) In the case of danger for the environment:

  (i) the risk phrases corresponding to the classification category dangerous for the environment (these phrases must appear on the label).

142 For ***preparations*** the risk phrases that appear on the label should be selected according to the following criteria and priorities:

(a) In the case of dangers which give rise to health effects:

  (i) the risk phrases which correspond to the category of danger illustrated by the overriding symbol. In certain cases the risk phrases should be adapted according to the tables in Part II of Schedule 3 of the CHIP Regulations. More specifically, the risk phrases of the constituent(s) which are responsible for the assignment of the preparation to the overriding danger category must appear on the label;

  (ii) risk phrases which correspond to the other categories of danger that have been attributed to the constituents but which are not illustrated by the overriding symbol;

(b) In the case of dangers arising from physico-chemical properties:

  (i) the criteria described under (a) are applicable, except that the risk phrases 'extremely flammable' or 'highly flammable' need not be indicated where they repeat the wording of the indication of danger used with a symbol.

143 As a general rule applying to substances and preparations, a maximum of four risk phrases should suffice to describe the risk (although in some cases the obligation to use certain risk phrases may result in more than four risk phrases being used). For this purpose the combined phrases listed in Part III of the Approved Supply List should be regarded as single phrases. The risk phrases should cover all the principal hazards associated with the preparation. However if the supplier feels there is a need to identify environmental hazards, additional risk phrases should be added as required.

Safety phrases

144 The wording of safety phrases should comply with that laid down in Part IV of Volume 1 of the Approved Supply List. The combined safety phrases should be used where applicable.

145 For substances appearing in the Approved Supply List, the safety phrases should be those shown in the Approved Supply List. Where no safety phrases are shown the supplier may include any appropriate safety phrase.

146 The final choice of safety phrases should have regard to the risk phrases indicated on the label and to the intended use of the substance or preparation:

(a) as a general rule, a maximum of four safety phrases shall suffice to formulate the most appropriate safety advice (although in some cases the obligation to use certain safety phrases will result in more than four safety phrases being used). For this purpose the combined phrases listed in the Approved Supply List shall be regarded as single phrases;

(b) in the case of danger to the environment a minimum of one and a maximum of four safety phrases should be used;

(c) some risk phrases become superfluous if a careful selection is made of safety phrases and vice-versa. Safety phrases which obviously correspond to risk phrases should appear on the label only if it is intended to emphasise a specific warning.

(d) particular attention should be given, in the choice of safety phrases, to the foreseen conditions of use of certain substances and preparations, eg spraying or other aerosol effects. Phrases should be chosen with the intended use in view;

(e) the safety phrases S1, S2 and S45 are obligatory for all very toxic, toxic and corrosive substances and preparations sold to the general public.

(f) the safety phrases S2 and S46 are obligatory for all other dangerous substances and preparations sold to the general public (except those substances classified as dangerous for the environment).

Final choice of risk and safety phrases

147 Although the final choice of the most appropriate risk and safety phrases is primarily governed by the need to give all necessary information, consideration should also be given to the clarity and impact of the label. With clarity in mind, the necessary information should be expressed in a minimum number of phrases.

NB Regulation 9(7) of CHIP allows some derogations for certain substances and preparations which are supplied in quantities of 125 ml or less.

Other information to be provided on the label

148 For substances, the information is completed by the name of the substance, the EEC number, and the name, address and telephone number of the person established in the Community who is responsible for placing the substance on the market.

149 For substances listed in the Approved Supply List the name on the label should be one of those given in the list for that substance. For substances not

shown in the Approved Supply List, the name should be the one used in the European Inventory of Existing Commercial Substances (EINECS), or the European List of Notified Chemical Substances (ELINCS), or, if it is not so listed, an internationally recognised name.

150 For preparations, the information is completed by the designation or the trade name of the preparation, the chemical names of the substances present in the preparation (paragraph 2 in Part I of Schedule 6 of the CHIP Regulations) and the name, address and telephone number of the person established in the Community who is responsible for placing the preparation on the market.

Note: In the case of concentrate preparations which are intended for the perfume industry and which may be sensitisers:

(a) the person responsible for placing them on the market may identify merely the one sensitising substance judged by him to be primarily responsible for the sensitisation hazard;

(b) in the case of a natural substance, the chemical name may be of the type: 'essential oil of . . . ', 'extract of . . .', rather than the name of the constituents of that essential oil or extract.

151 Certain preparations attract additional labelling requirements as set out in regulation 10 and Part II of Schedule 6 of the CHIP Regulations.

Special cases

Mobile gas cylinders

152 For mobile gas cylinders the requirements concerning labelling are considered to be satisfied when they are in agreement with regulations 9 and 11 of CHIP, including the arrangements for combined carriage and supply labelling. However, by way of derogation from regulations 11(2), (4) and (5) of CHIP, one of the following alternatives can be used for gas cylinders with a water capacity of less than or equal to 150 litres:

(a) the format and dimensions of the label can follow the prescriptions of the ISO Standard ISO/DP 7225, in which case, for preparations, the label can bear the generic name or industrial (commercial) name of the preparation provided the dangerous component substances of the preparation are shown on the body of the gas cylinder in a clear and indelible way; or

(b) the information specified in regulation 9(2) or 9(3) of CHIP may be provided on a durable information disc or label held captive on the cylinder.

Gas containers intended for propane, butane or liquefied petroleum gas (LPG) or for preparations containing stenched propane, butane or LPG

153 Propane, butane and liquefied petroleum gas are classified in the Approved Supply List. Although these substances (and preparations containing these substances) are classified as hazardous in accordance with regulation 5 of CHIP, they do not present a danger to human health when they are placed on the market in closed refillable cylinders or in non-refillable cartridges within the scope of EN 417 as fuel gases which are only released for combustion.

154 These cylinders or cartridges must be labelled with the appropriate symbol and the R- and S-phrases concerning flammability. No information concerning the effects on human health is required on the label. However, the information concerning effects on human health which should have appeared on the label shall be transmitted to the professional user by the person responsible for placing the substance on the market by way of a safety data sheet. For the consumer, sufficient information shall be transmitted to enable them to take all necessary measures for health and safety as described in regulation 6(5) of CHIP.

Substances and preparations classified with R65

155 Substances and preparations classified as harmful on the basis of an aspiration hazard need not be labelled as harmful with R65 when placed on the market in aerosol containers or in containers fitted with a sealed spray attachment.

Metals in massive form

156 If not already classified in the Approved Supply List, these substances should be classified in accordance with regulation 5(4) of CHIP. Some of these substances, however, although correctly classified, do not present a danger to human health by inhalation, ingestion or contact with the skin in the form in which they are supplied. Such substances do not require a label under regulation 9 of CHIP. However, all the information which should have appeared on the label should be transmitted by the supplier to the user. In general this information will be in the form of a safety data sheet.

Gaseous preparations (gas mixtures)

157 For gaseous preparations, consideration should be given to the evaluation of:

(a) physico-chemical properties;

(b) health hazards.

Evaluation of physico-chemical properties

Flammability

158 The flammable properties of these preparations should be determined in accordance with paragraph 3 in Part I of Schedule 3 of the CHIP Regulations. Gaseous preparations should be classified according to the results of the relevant tests in Annex V of Directive 67/548/EEC and the criteria in this Approved Guide. By way of derogation, however, where these preparations are produced to order in small quantities, the flammability of these gaseous mixtures can be evaluated by the following calculation method.

159 A gaseous mixture may be represented as:

$$A_1F_1 + ... + A_iF_i + ... A_nF_n + B_1I_1 + ... B_iI_i + ... B_pI_p$$

where: A_i and B_i are the molar fractions
F_i flammable gas
I_i inert gas
n number of flammable gases
p number of inert gases

160 This can also be expressed in a form where all the I_i (inert gases) are replaced by a nitrogen equivalent using a coefficient of equivalency, K_i. The equivalent concentration of a flammable gas A'_i, is then expressed as follows:

$$A'_i = A_i \times \left(\frac{100}{A_i + K_i B_i}\right)$$

161 The maximum concentration of flammable gases (Tci) which, when mixed with nitrogen, gives a concentration that is not flammable in air can be expressed as:

$$\sum{}_i A'_i / Tci \leq 1$$

If the value of the above expression is greater than one, the gas mixture is flammable and the preparation should be classified as extremely flammable and the risk phrase R12 should be assigned.

162 The values of the coefficients of equivalency (K_i) between the inert gases and nitrogen and the values of the maximum content of flammable gas (Tci) may be found in Tables 1 and 2 of ISO Standard ISO/DIS 10156. When a Tci value for a flammable gas does not appear in this standard, the corresponding lower explosivity limit (LEL) should be used. If no LEL value exists, the value of Tci should be set at 1% by volume.

163 The expression in paragraph 161 can be used to derive appropriate labelling of gaseous preparations. It should be noted, however, that the expression:

(a) should not be regarded as a substitute for the determination of technical safety parameters by experimental methods;

(b) does not take into account the effects of oxidising gases on the mixture and therefore should not be used to check whether such a gas mixture can be prepared safely;

(c) will not give reliable results if the individual gases interfere with each other to affect the flammability of the mixture. An example of such interference is the effect of adding a halogenated hydrocarbon to a flammable gas.

Oxidising properties

164 As Annex V of Directive 67/548/EEC does not contain a method to determine the oxidising properties of gaseous mixtures, these properties should be estimated by comparing the oxidising potential of gases in a mixture with that of oxygen in air. A gas mixture is considered to be equally or more oxidising than air if:

$$\sum{}_i x_i \, C_i \geq 21$$

where: x_i is the concentration of gas i in vol %
C_i is the coefficient of oxygen equivalency

In this case, the preparation is classified as oxidising and the phrase R8 should be assigned.

165 The coefficients of oxygen equivalency are listed in ISO Standard ISO/DIS 10156. They are:

O_2	1
N_2O	0.6

When no value for the C_i coefficient is given in this standard a value of 40 should be assigned.

Evaluation of the health effects

166 The evaluation of the dangers of a preparation for health should be made according to Schedule 3 of the CHIP Regulations. Where evaluation of the health hazards is made according to the conventional method the appropriate individual concentration limits are expressed in per cent by volume and appear either in the Approved Supply List for the gas(es) considered, or in Part II of Schedule 3 of the CHIP Regulations when the gas(es) considered are not in the Approved Supply List, or appear there without concentration limits.

Alloys, preparations containing polymers, preparations containing elastomers

167 These preparations should be classified and labelled according to the requirements of CHIP. Some of these preparations, however, although properly classified under Schedule 3 of the CHIP Regulations do not present a danger to human health by inhalation, ingestion or contact with skin in the form in which they are supplied. Such preparations do not require a label under regulation 9 of CHIP. However all the information which would have appeared on the label should be transmitted to the user by means of the supplier's safety data sheet.

Organic peroxides

168 Organic peroxides combine the properties of an oxidiser to an oxidiser and a combustible substance in one molecule: when an organic peroxide decomposes, the oxidising part of the molecule reacts exothermically with the combustible (oxidisable) part. For the oxidising properties the existing methods in Directive 92/62/EEC cannot be applied to organic peroxides. The following calculation method based on the presence of active oxygen must be used.

169 The available oxygen content (%) of an organic peroxide preparation is given by the formula:

16 x (ni x ci/mi)

where:

ni = number of peroxygen groups per molecule of organic peroxide i,
ci = concentration (mass %) of organic peroxide i,
mi = molecular mass of organic peroxide i.

Appendix 1 Safety phrases for substances and preparations

Safety phrases should be assigned to dangerous substances and preparations in accordance with the general criteria below. In addition, for certain preparations safety advice is given in regulation 10 and Part II of Schedule 6 of CHIP. References to the manufacturer include any supplier.

S1 *Keep locked up*

Applicability:

- Very toxic and toxic and corrosive substances and preparations.

Criteria for use:

- *Obligatory* for those substances and preparations mentioned above if sold to the general public.

S2 *Keep out of the reach of children*

Applicability:

- All dangerous substances and preparations.

Criteria for use:

- *Obligatory* only for all dangerous substances and preparations sold to the general public, except for those only classified as dangerous for the environment.

S3 *Keep in a cool place*

Applicability:

- Organic peroxides.
- Other dangerous substances and preparations having a boiling point ≤40°C.

Criteria for use:

- *Obligatory* for organic peroxides unless S47 is used.
- Recommended for other dangerous substances and preparations having a boiling point ≤ 40°C.

S4 *Keep away from living quarters*

Applicability:

- Very toxic and toxic substances and preparations.

Criteria for use:

- Normally limited to very toxic and toxic substances and preparations when desirable to supplement S13; for example when there is an inhalation risk and the substance or preparation should be stored away from living quarters. The advice is not intended to preclude proper use of the substance or preparation in living quarters.

S5 *Keep contents under . . .*
(appropriate liquid to be specified by the manufacturer)

Applicability:

- Spontaneously flammable solid substances and preparations.

Criteria for use:

- Normally limited to special cases, eg sodium, potassium or white phosphorous.

S6 *Keep under . . .*
(inert gas to be specified by the manufacturer)

Applicability:

- Dangerous substances and preparations which must be kept under an inert atmosphere.

Criteria for use:

- Normally limited to special cases, eg certain organo-metallic compounds.

S7 *Keep container tightly closed*

Applicability:

- Organic peroxides.

- Substances and preparations which can give off very toxic, toxic, harmful or extremely flammable gases.

- Substances and preparations which on contact with moisture give off extremely flammable gases.

- Highly flammable solids.

Criteria for use:

- *Obligatory* for organic peroxides.

- Recommended for other fields of application mentioned above.

S8 *Keep container dry*

Applicability:

- Substances and preparations which may react violently with water.

- Substances and preparations which on contact with water liberate extremely flammable gases.

- Substances and preparations which on contact with water liberate very toxic or toxic gases.

Criteria for use:

- Normally limited to the fields of application mentioned above when necessary to reinforce warnings given by R14, R15 in particular, and R29.

S9 *Keep container in a well-ventilated place*

Applicability:

- Volatile substances and preparations which may give off very toxic, toxic or harmful vapours.

- Extremely flammable or highly flammable liquids and extremely flammable gases.

Criteria for use:

- Recommended for volatile substances and preparations which may give off very toxic, toxic or harmful vapours.

- Recommended for extremely flammable or highly flammable liquids or extremely flammable gases.

S12 *Do not keep the container sealed*

Applicability:

- Substances and preparations which will be giving off gases or vapours liable to burst the container.

Criteria for use:

- Normally limited to special cases mentioned above.

S13 *Keep away from food, drink and animal feedingstuffs*

Applicability:

- Very toxic, toxic and harmful substances and preparations.

Criteria for use:

- Recommended when such substances and preparations are likely to be used by the general public.

S14 *Keep away from . . .*
(incompatible materials to be indicated by the manufacturer)

Applicability:

- Organic peroxides.

Criteria for use:

- *Obligatory* for and normally limited to organic peroxides. However, may be useful in exceptional cases when incompatibility is likely to produce a particular risk.

S15 *Keep away from heat*

Applicability:

- Substances and preparations which may decompose or which may react spontaneously under the effect of heat.

Criteria for use:

- Normally limited to special cases, eg monomers, but not assigned if risk phrases R2, R3 and/or R5 have already been applied.

S16 *Keep away from sources of ignition - No smoking*

Applicability:

- Extremely flammable or highly flammable liquids and extremely flammable gases.

Criteria for use:

- Recommended for the substances and preparations mentioned above but not assigned if risk phrases R2, R3 and/or R5 have already been applied.

S17 *Keep away from combustible material*

Applicability:

- Substances and preparations which may form explosive or spontaneously flammable mixtures with combustible material.

Criteria for use:

- Available for use in special cases (eg to emphasise R8 and R9).

S18 *Handle and open container with care*

Applicability:

- Substances and preparations liable to produce an overpressure in the container.

- Substances and preparations which may form explosive peroxides.

Criteria for use:

- Normally limited to the above-mentioned cases when there is risk of damage to the eyes and/or when the substances and preparations are likely to be used by the general public.

S20 *When using do not eat or drink*

Applicability:

- Very toxic, toxic and corrosive substances and preparations.

Criteria for use:

- Normally limited to special cases (eg arsenic and arsenic compounds; fluoracetates) in particular when any of these are likely to be used by the general public.

S21 *When using do not smoke*

Applicability:

- Substances and preparations which produce toxic products on combustion.

Criteria for use:

- Normally limited to special cases (eg halogenated compounds).

S22 *Do not breathe dust*

Applicability:

- All solid dangerous substances and preparations dangerous to health.

Criteria for use:

- *Obligatory* for those substances and preparations mentioned above to which R42 is assigned.
- Recommended for those substances and preparations mentioned above which are supplied in the form of an inhalable dust and for which the health hazards following inhalation are not known.

S23 *Do not breath gas/fumes/vapour/spray*
(appropriate wording to be specified by the manufacturer)

Applicability:

- All liquid or gaseous substances and preparations dangerous to health.

Criteria for use:

- *Obligatory* for those substances and preparations mentioned above R42 is assigned.
- *Obligatory* for substances and preparations intended for use by spraying. Either S38 or S51 must be ascribed in addition.
- Recommended when it is necessary to draw the attention of the user to inhalation risks not mentioned in the risk phrases which have to be ascribed.

S24 *Avoid contact with skin*

Applicability:

- All substances and preparations dangerous to health.

Criteria for use:

- *Obligatory* for those substances and preparations to which R43 has been ascribed unless S36 has also been ascribed.
- Recommended when it is necessary to draw the attention of the user to skin contact risks not mentioned in the risk phrases which have to be ascribed. However, may be used to emphasise such risk phrases.

S25 *Avoid contact with eyes*

Applicability:

- Corrosive or irritant substances and preparations.

Criteria for use:

- Normally limited to special cases, ie when it is considered essential to emphasise the risk to eyes denoted by use of R34, R35, R36 or R41. Thus important if these substances and preparations are likely to be used by the general public and eye or face protection may not be available.

S26 *In case of contact with eyes, rinse immediately with plenty of water and seek medical advice*

Applicability:

- Corrosive or irritant substances and preparations.

Criteria for use:

- *Obligatory* for corrosive substances and preparations and those to which R41 has already been ascribed.

- Recommended for irritant substances to which the risk phrase R36 has already been ascribed.

S27 *Take off immediately all contaminated clothing*

Applicability:

- Very toxic, toxic or corrosive substances and preparations.

Criteria for use:

- Recommended for very toxic and toxic substances and preparations which are easily absorbed by the skin and for corrosive substances and preparations. However this safety phrase should not be used if S36 has been ascribed.

S28 *After contact with skin, wash immediately with plenty of . . .* (to be specified by the manufacturer)

Applicability:

- Very toxic, toxic or corrosive substances and preparations.

Criteria for use:

- *Obligatory* for very toxic substances and preparations.

- Recommended for the other substances and preparations mentioned above, in particular when water is not the most appropriate rinsing fluid.

S29 *Do not empty into drains*

Applicability:

- Extremely or highly flammable liquids immiscible with water.

Criteria for use:

- Recommended for above mentioned substances and preparations which are likely to be used by the general public.

S30 *Never add water to this product*

Applicability:

- Substances and preparations which react violently with water.

Criteria for use:

- Normally limited to special cases (eg sulphuric acid) and may be used, as appropriate, to give the clearest possible information, either to emphasise R14 or as an alternative to R14.

S33 *Take precautionary measures against static discharges*

Applicability:

- Extremely or highly flammable substances and preparations.

Criteria for use:

- Recommended for substances and preparations used in industry which do not absorb moisture. Virtually never used for substances and preparations as placed on the market for use by the general public.

S35 *This material and its container must be disposed of in a safe way*

Applicability:

- Explosive substances and preparations.

- Very toxic and toxic substances and preparations.

- Substances dangerous for the environment.

Criteria for use:

- *Obligatory* for explosive substances and preparations other than organic peroxides.

- Recommended for very toxic and toxic substances and preparations, particularly when likely to be used by the general public.

- Recommended for substances dangerous for the environment for which S56 does not apply when such substances are likely to be used by the general public.

S36 *Wear suitable protective clothing*

Applicability:

- Organic peroxides.

- Very toxic, toxic or harmful substances and preparations.

- Corrosive substances and preparations.

Criteria for use:

- *Obligatory* for very toxic and corrosive substances and preparations.

- *Obligatory* for those substances and preparations to which either R21 or R24 has been ascribed.

- *Obligatory* for Category 3 carcinogens, mutagens and substances toxic to reproduction unless the effects are produced solely by inhalation of the substance or preparation.

- *Obligatory* for organic peroxides.

- Recommended for toxic substances and preparations if the LD50 dermal value is unknown but the substance or preparation is likely to be toxic through skin contact.

- Recommended for substances and preparations used in industry which are liable to damage health by prolonged exposure.

S37 *Wear suitable gloves*

Applicability:

- Very toxic, toxic, harmful or corrosive substances and preparations.

- Organic peroxides.

- Substances and preparations irritating to the skin.

Criteria for use:

- *Obligatory* for very toxic and corrosive substances and preparations.

- *Obligatory* for those substances and preparations to which either R21, R24 or R43 has been ascribed.

- *Obligatory* for Category 3 carcinogens, mutagens and substances toxic to reproduction unless the effects are produced solely by inhalation of the substance or preparation.
- *Obligatory* for organic peroxides.

- Recommended for toxic substances and preparations if the LD50 dermal value is unknown but the substance or preparation is likely to be toxic through skin contact.

- Recommended for substances and preparations which are irritating to the skin because of their defatting properties.

S38 *In case of insufficient ventilation wear suitable respiratory equipment*

Applicability:

- Very toxic or toxic substances and preparations.

Criteria for use:

- Normally limited to special cases involving the use of very toxic or toxic substances and preparations in industry or in agriculture.

S39 *Wear eye/face protection*

Applicability:

- Organic peroxides.

- Corrosive substances and preparations, including irritants which give rise to risk of serious damage to the eyes.

- Very toxic and toxic substances and preparations.

Criteria for use:

- *Obligatory* for those substances and preparations to which R34, R 35 or R 41 have been ascribed.

- *Obligatory* for organic peroxides.

- Recommended when it is necessary to draw the attention of the user to eye contact risks not mentioned in the risk phrases which have to be ascribed.

- Normally limited to exceptional cases for very toxic and toxic substances and preparations, where there is a risk of splashing and they are likely to be easily absorbed by the skin.

S40 *To clean the floor and all objects contaminated by this material use . . .* (to be specified by the manufacturer)

Applicability:

- All dangerous substances and preparations.

Criteria for use:

- Normally limited to those dangerous substances and preparations for which water is not considered to be a suitable cleansing agent (eg where absorption by powdered material, dissolution by solvent etc is necessary) and where it is important for health and/or safety reasons to provide a warning on the label.

S41 *In case of fire and/or explosion do not breathe fumes*

Applicability:

- Dangerous substances and preparations which on combustion give off very toxic or toxic gases.

Criteria for use:

- Normally limited to special cases.

S42 *During fumigation/spraying wear suitable respiratory equipment* (appropriate wording to be specified by the manufacturer)

Applicability:

- Substances and preparations intended for such use but which may endanger the health and safety of the user unless proper precautions are taken.

Criteria for use:

- Normally limited to special cases.

S43 *In case of fire use . . .*
(indicate in the space the precise type of fire-fighting equipment. If water increases the risk add: *Never use water*)

Applicability:

- Extremely flammable, highly flammable and flammable substances and preparations.

Criteria for use:

- *Obligatory* for substances and preparations which in contact with water or damp air, evolve extremely flammable gases.
- Recommended for extremely flammable, highly flammable and flammable substances and preparations, particularly when they are immiscible with water.

S45 *In case of accident or if you feel unwell seek medical advice immediately (show the label where possible)*

Applicability:

- Very toxic substances and preparations.
- Toxic and corrosive substances and preparations.

Criteria for use:

- *Obligatory* for the substances and preparations mentioned above.

S46 *If swallowed, seek medical advice immediately and show this container or label*

Applicability:

- All dangerous substances and preparations other than those which are very toxic, toxic, corrosive or dangerous to the environment.

Criteria for use:

- *Obligatory* for all dangerous substances and preparations mentioned above which are likely to be used by the general public, unless there is no reason to fear any danger from swallowing, particularly by children.

S47 *Keep at temperature not exceeding . . . ^{o}C*
(to be specified by the manufacturer)

Applicability:

- Substances and preparations which become unstable at a certain temperature.

Criteria for use:

- Normally limited to special cases (eg certain organic peroxides).

S48 *Keep wetted with . . .*
(appropriate material to be specified by the manufacturer)

Applicability:

- Substances and preparations which may become very sensitive to sparks, friction or impact if allowed to dry out.

Criteria for use:

- Normally limited to special cases, eg nitrocelluloses.

S49 *Keep only in the original container*

Applicability:

- Substances and preparations sensitive to catalytic decomposition.

Criteria for use:

- Substances and preparations sensitive to catalytic decomposition, eg certain organic peroxides.

S50 *Do not mix with . . .*
(to be specified by the manufacturer)

Applicability:

- Substances and preparations which may react with the specified product to evolve very toxic or toxic gases.

- Organic peroxides.

Criteria for use:

- Recommended for substances and preparations mentioned above which are likely to be used by members of the general public, when it is a better alternative to R31 or R32.
- *Obligatory* with certain peroxides which may give violent reaction with accelerators or promoters.

S51 *Use only in well-ventilated areas*

Applicability:

- Substances and preparations likely to or intended to produce vapours, dusts, sprays, fumes, mists, etc which give rise to inhalation risks or to a fire or explosion risk.

Criteria for use:

- Recommended when use of S38 would not be appropriate. Thus important when such substances and preparations are likely to be used by the general public.

S52 *Not recommended for interior use on large surface areas*

Applicability:

- Volatile very toxic, toxic and harmful substances and preparations containing them.

Criteria for use:

- Recommended when damage to health is likely to be caused by prolonged exposure to these substances by reason of their volatilisation from large treated surfaces in the home or other enclosed places where people congregate.

S53 *Avoid exposure - Obtain special instructions before use*

Applicability:

- Substances and preparations that are carcinogenic, mutagenic and/or toxic to reproduction.

Criteria for use:

- *Obligatory* for the above-mentioned substances and preparations to which at least one of the following risk phrases has been assigned: R45, R46, R49, R60 or R61.

S56 *Dispose of this material and its container to hazardous or special waste collection point*

Applicability:

- Substances dangerous for the environment.

Criteria for use:

- Recommended for substances which have been assigned the symbol 'N' and which are likely to be used by the general public.

S57 *Use appropriate containment to avoid environmental contamination*

Applicability:

- Substances which have been assigned the symbol 'N'.

Criteria for use:

- Normally limited to substances not likely to be used by the general public.

S59 *Refer to manufacturer/supplier for information on recovery/recycling*

Applicability:

- Substances dangerous for the environment.

Criteria for use:

- *Obligatory* for substances dangerous for the ozone layer.

- Recommended for other substances assigned the symbol 'N' and for which recovery/recycling is recommended.

S60 *This material and its container must be disposed of as hazardous waste*

Applicability:

- Substances dangerous for the environment.

Criteria for use:

- Recommended for substances which have been assigned the symbol 'N' not likely to be used by the general public.

S61 *Avoid release to the environment. Refer to special instructions/safety data sheet*

Applicability:

- Substances dangerous for the environment.

Criteria for use:

- Normally used for substances which have been assigned the symbol 'N'.

- Recommended for all substances classified dangerous for the environment not covered above.

S62 *If swallowed, do not induce vomiting: seek medical advice immediately and show this container or label*

Applicability:

- Substances and preparations classified as harmful with R65 in accordance with the criteria in paragraph 48.

- Not applicable to substances or preparations which are placed on the market in aerosol containers (or in containers. fitted with a sealed spray attachment). See paragraph 155 (Substances and preparations classified with R65).

Criteria for use:

- *Obligatory* for substances and preparations mentioned above, if sold to, or likely to be used by the general public.

- Recommended for the substances and preparations mentioned above when used in industry.

Appendix 2 Notice of Approval adopting the revised Annex V of the Dangerous Substances Directive (67/548/EEC) as an Approved Code of Practice

By virtue of section 16(1) of the Health and Safety at Work etc Act 1974 and with the consent of the Secretary of State for the Environment the Health and Safety Commission has on 6 June 1997 adopted as an Approved Code of Practice Annex V to EC Directive 67/548/EEC,* as amended by EC Directive 96/54/EC.†

The Code of Practice gives practical guidance on the tests for:

(i) new substances which may be required by the competent authority in accordance with Notification of New Substances Regulations 1993; and

(ii) the classification of preparations which may be required by the Health and Safety Executive in accordance with the Chemicals (Hazard Information and Packaging for Supply) Regulations 1994, as amended.**

The Code of Practice comes into effect on 7 July 1997.

Signed

T A GATES
Secretary to the Health and Safety Commission

6 June 1997

Notes (these footnotes do not form part of the Notice of Approval)

* Annex V of Directive 67/548/EEC is published as Directive 92/69/EC (the 17th Adaptation to technical progress of 67/548/EEC) in the Official Journal, 29 December 1992, L383. Annex V also includes Directive 87/302/EEC in part.

† 96/54/EC (the 22nd Adaptation to technical progress of 67/548/EEC) amends Annex V and is published in the Official Journal, 30 September 1996, L248.

** The Chemicals (Hazard Information and Packaging for Supply) Regulations 1994 have been amended by the Chemicals (Hazard Information and Packaging for Supply) (Amendment) Regulations 1996 and the Chemicals (Hazard Information and Packaging for Supply) (Amendment) Regulations 1997 and are collectively known as 'CHIP'.

Printed and published by the Health and Safety Executive 6/97 C120